The DATA Model Skills Checklist

Child's name:	Date of birth:
Parent(s)/guardian(s):	
First administration date:	Staff member(s) completing form:
Second administration date:	Staff member(s) completing form:
Child's preferred items and activities:	
Child's primary mode of communication:	

Directions:

1. This checklist is intended to be filled out at least twice during the school year. For each administration, use a different colored pen to differentiate between the two administration dates. For example, for the first administration use a blue pen, and for the second administration, use a red pen.
2. Several items are directly tested; others are observed and scored during classroom routines and activities. Adult instructions are provided for items to be directly tested. Scoring is as follows:

   2 = Consistently/always meets criterion

   1 = Inconsistently/sometimes meets criterion

   0 = Does not/never meet(s) criterion
3. After completing the checklist, put a * next to items that are priorities for learning, then fill out the *Priority skills* section at the end of this checklist with those items.

NOTES ______________________________

A. ADAPTIVE

1.	Mealtime	Scoring	Comments	*
1.1	Drinks from open cup *Brings open cup to mouth and returns cup to surface without spilling*	0 1 2		
1.2	Eats with fork or spoon *Spears or scoops food and brings to mouth with minimal spilling*	0 1 2		
1.3	Eats a variety of food *Discuss importance, level of priority with family before making an intervention plan*	0 1 2		
1.4	Remains at table during meals *Remains at table until asked to leave, adult excuses child, or until the natural end of the mealtime*	0 1 2		
2.	**Personal hygiene**	**Scoring**	**Comments**	*
2.1	Toilet trained—urine *Demonstrates bladder control, using the toilet to void. Adult may provide some assistance for clothing and occasional reminders are acceptable, as developmentally appropriate.*	0 1 2		
2.2	Toilet trained—bowel *Demonstrates bowel control, using the toilet to void. Adult may provide some assistance with clothing and occasional reminders are acceptable, as developmentally appropriate.*	0 1 2		
2.3	Washes and dries hands *Child is able to complete all steps of hand washing routine independently. Occasional reminders are acceptable as appropriate to age.*	0 1 2		
3.	**School skills**	**Scoring**	**Comments**	*
3.1	Manages personal belongings *When given a direction to get their own materials (e.g., lunchbox, backpack, coat) or during a transition in the schedule, the child is able to get and put away personal belongings needed for the activity.*	0 1 2		
3.2	Uses classroom materials *When given classroom materials such as scissors, markers, paper, etc., child is able to use materials appropriately. For example, child picks up scissors and attempts to cut with scissors.*	0 1 2		
3.3	Completes transitions between activities *When an activity is finished, child is able to clean up if needed, get materials for next activity, and line up and remain with group completing the transition.*	0 1 2		
3.4	Walks with peers in small or large groups across a variety of school settings *Walks in school building, school grounds, and in the community staying in pace with an adult. Child does not run off or need hand held for entire duration of walking activity.*	0 1 2		
3.5	Rides in school bus, car, or other transportation to and from school *Child is able to sit and remain in car seat or other appropriate seating with absence of protest for duration of trip.*	0 1 2		

3. School skills *(continued)*	Scoring	Comments	*
3.6 Waits for instruction to begin (individual, small group, large group) *Child is able to wait quietly and remain seated or standing until the teacher provides the direction for the activity.*	0 1 2		
3.7 Works independently on a teacher selected activity *Child is able to sit and attend to a nonpreferred activity until completion.*	0 1 2		
3.8 Begins and completes at least three different teacher selected activities *Teacher prepares activities and child will complete them with only a few reminders or directions.*	0 1 2		
3.9 Participates in a group activity for:	0 1 2		
■ 5 minutes	0 1 2		
■ 10 minutes	0 1 2		
■ 15 minutes	0 1 2		
Participation includes attending to materials and teacher, acting on the materials if required, remaining with the group until natural end of activity. Group activities may include but are not limited to both small and large group, transitions with the group, and lunch or snack.			
4. Self-Advocacy	**Scoring**	**Comments**	*****
4.1 Requests a break when needed *Child makes request for a break before leaving area or room.*	0 1 2		
4.2 Protests *During a nonpreferred activity or offered a less preferred item, the child will communicate, "No," "No thank you," "I don't want that," or "I'm done," either verbally or nonverbally.*	0 1 2		
4.3 Requests help from adults and peers when needed *When child needs help, he or she will do so with a calm body.*	0 1 2		
4.4 Requests clarification when needed *Child may ask the adult to repeat the direction, state that he or she doesn't know what to do, etc.*	0 1 2		
4.5 Asks for accommodations *For example, may ask to see pictures or a schedule, may ask for another minute to finish activity.*	0 1 2		
4.6 Identify likes and dislikes *Child will state at least four different items he/she likes and four different items he/she dislikes, such as food, toys, color.*	0 1 2		
4.7 States identifying information about self *When asked identifying information such as "What is your name?" or "How old are you?" child will respond correctly across at least four different identifying items.*	0 1 2		

5. **Behaviors that interfere with participation and learning**		
The purpose of this section is to identify behaviors that have been resistant to ongoing classroom instruction and behavioral support. The purpose is not to identify all behaviors the child may demonstrate, only those that are chronic and interfere with instruction.		
Example: Screaming	(Yes) No	Context: Child screams when asked to do a nonpreferred activity. This only happens with one of the teachers in the classroom.
Aggression	Yes No	Context:
Self-injurious behavior	Yes No	Context:
Property destruction	Yes No	Context:
Running away	Yes No	Context:
Self-stimulatory behavior	Yes No	Context:
Screaming	Yes No	Context:
Noncompliance	Yes No	Context:
Other	Yes No	Context:
Other	Yes No	Context:
Other	Yes No	Context:
Summary notes for adaptive		

B. EXECUTIVE FUNCTIONING

DATA

1. **Flexibility**	Scoring	Comments	*
1.1 Follows classroom routine and schedule *Child references posted schedule in classroom or follows teacher's directions to transition to another activity with a calm body.*	0 1 2		
1.2 Accepts interruptions or unexpected change *Child may verbally or nonverbally, appropriately express displeasure with change, but is able to accept change or interruptions and move on.*	0 1 2		
1.3 Accepts being told "no" without becoming upset or angry *When the child is told that he or she cannot have the object or activity, child accepts this response without becoming upset as age appropriate.*	0 1 2		
1.4 Relinquishes preferred toy, food, or materials to an adult or peer when asked *Child may receive adult reminder or support, but will relinquish item without protest or with appropriate protest (e.g., "I don't want to." or "wait.").*	0 1 2		
1.5 Accepts that things don't go as expected *During a group game the child does not have the first turn, does not protest, and will participate in the game.* *If a child does not finish first in the game, they do not protest, may say, "That's okay . . . maybe next time" or congratulate the winner.* *If a child is drawing a picture and makes an unintended mark, the child does not rip up his or her paper.*	0 1 2		
2. **Self-Regulation: Self and emotional control**	**Scoring**	**Comments**	*
2.1 Waits for a preferred item or activity *When child is told to wait, he or she will wait quietly and calmly for the item.*	0 1 2		
2.2 Accepts comfort from others if upset or agitated *Allows caregiver or familiar adult to give them a hug or peers to pat their back.*	0 1 2		
2.3 Self-regulates when tense or upset with verbal or visual cue *For example, calms self by counting to 10, taking a breath, taking a break, etc.*	0 1 2		
2.4 Self-regulates when energy level is high or low with verbal or visual cue *If energy level is high, the child may count to 10 or squeeze a squishy ball. If energy level is low, the child may walk around the room or jump on a trampoline*	0 1 2		
3. **Persistence, organization, and time management**	**Scoring**	**Comments**	*
3.1 Persists in gaining a person's attention *Child will call a person's name or tap that person until the person acknowledges the child.*	0 1 2		
3.2 Persists, or continues to try, when something is difficult *The child is trying to put a toy together, and the pieces don't fit, but they persist in trying to put the pieces together.*	0 1 2		

3. Persistence, organization, and time management (*continued*)	Scoring	Comments	*
3.3 Follows a sequence of at least three steps in an activity *For example, when given verbal or visual steps in a sequence, child will complete the activity in order by following the direction or referencing the picture sequence.*	0 1 2		
3.4 Finishes an activity within a timely manner, cleans up, and moves to the next activity *Consider developmentally appropriate time which may be indicated by the child completing the activity when other children of the same age in the classroom complete the activity.*	0 1 2		
4. Problem solving	**Scoring**	**Comments**	*
4.1 Claims and defends possessions *For example, if a peer takes the child's trading cards, the child will try to hold on to them or say, "That's mine."*	0 1 2		
4.2 Identifies or defines the problem *If two children want the same toy, the child will communicate that the problem is two children want one toy.*	0 1 2		
4.3 Generates solutions *If an art project rips, the child may suggest getting tape to fix it or make a new one.*	0 1 2		
4.4 Carries out solutions by negotiating or compromising *Two children want the same toy and the child suggests they take turns, do eeney-meaney-miney-mo or set a timer to show when a turn is over.*	0 1 2		
5. Emotional knowledge	**Scoring**	**Comments**	*
5.1 Identifies simple emotions in pictures and books *When presented with different emotions in pictures or books and asked, "Which one is happy," child will point to, give, or tap the picture. If asked, "How does she feel," child will state, "She is happy."*	0 1 2		
5.2 Labels and identifies emotions in self *If their toy breaks, and the child is sad, they can label that emotion accurately when asked, "How do you feel?"*	0 1 2		
5.3 Labels and identifies emotions in others *If a peer is angry, the child will be able to say, "He is mad."*	0 1 2		
5.4 Justifies an emotion once identified/labeled *If a girl is crying the child can say she is crying because she fell down and is hurt.*	0 1 2		
5.5 Demonstrates affection and empathy toward peers *Gives hugs or handshakes to peers and asks if a peer is okay when appropriate.*	0 1 2		

Summary notes for executive functioning

1. **Imitation**	Scoring	Comments	*
1.1 Imitates actions with objects *Imitates five common actions and five novel actions with objects (e.g., place block on block, shake maraca, push car, pull toy, squeeze toy, scribble, drink from a cup, feed a doll)*	0 1 2		
1.2 Imitates large motor movements *Imitates five actions that are visible to the child (that the child can see themselves perform such as wave, clap hands, and tap legs) and five that are not (e.g., arms up, shake head no, arms out to side, cover face such as peek-a-boo, touch nose, turn around)*	0 1 2		
1.3 Imitates fine motor movements *Imitates three different actions (e.g., open and close hands, extend index finger as in a point, wiggle fingers, thumbs up, squeeze clay or squeaky toy, pinch clothespin)*	0 1 2		
1.4 Imitates words *Child imitates frequently used, novel, and developmentally appropriate sounds and words.*	0 1 2		
1.5 Imitates multistep sequences *Imitates multistep actions or phrases while following along with teacher in a group setting (e.g., repeat after me songs or rhymes, action songs)*	0 1 2		
2. **Matching and categorizing**	**Scoring**	**Comments**	*****
2.1 Matches identical objects *Matches six different objects from an array of at least three*	0 1 2		
2.2 Matches identical pictures *Matches six different pictures or photos from an array of at least three*	0 1 2		
2.3 Matches objects to pictures *Matches six different objects to pictures from an array of at least three*	0 1 2		
2.4 Matches pictures to objects *Matches three different pictures to objects from an array of at least three*	0 1 2		
2.5 Matches nonidentical objects/pictures *Matches six different objects/pictures from at least three different categories (e.g., cars, foods, blocks) from an array of at least three*	0 1 2		
2.6 Groups objects according to:			
■ Size	0 1 2		
■ Shape	0 1 2		
■ Color	0 1 2		
Groups at least three objects for each attribute—size, shape, and color			
2.7 Groups functionally related objects *Puts together at least three objects that are functionally related across six different groups (for painting—child gathers paint, brush, paper; to play in a sandbox child gets bucket, shovel, and sifter)*	0 1 2		

2. Matching and categorizing (*continued*)	Scoring	Comments	*
2.8 Categorizes like objects *Puts together at least three objects in a group according to a broad-based category (e.g., food, clothing, animals; child gathers all toy animals together, puts play dishes and utensil on table, gathers clothing in order to play dress-up). Must group items for at least six different categories*	0 1 2		
3. Sequencing	**Scoring**	**Comments**	*****
3.1 Makes simple patterns *Child replicates, extends, and creates simple a-b-a-b patterns (e.g., makes a pattern of train, car, train, car, or with colored Legos does red, yellow, red, yellow).*	0 1 2		
3.2 Places objects from a continuum in order			
■ Size	0 1 2		
■ Part to whole *When given at least three objects to place in a series, child orders the items with at least three different examples.*	0 1 2		
3.3 Sequences pictures to tell a story *Child sequences at least four pictures in the correct order across at least four different types of sequences (e.g., washing hands, making a sandwich).*	0 1 2		
3.4 Recalls and retells past events *Child recalls at least three events and tells about each event in the correct order.*	0 1 2		
4. Emergent literacy	**Scoring**	**Comments**	*****
4.1 Makes comments and asks questions while looking at picture books *Child uses gesture and/or words to share or obtain information about pictures and text in books (e.g., child points to red balloon; says, "Look at balloon"; or asks, "Where's the mouse?"*	0 1 2		
4.2 Answers factual questions at the end of a familiar story *At the end of the story, child can answer factual questions about the main idea, main characters, or main events in the story.*	0 1 2		
4.3 Answers questions related to a story that requires inference *Child is able to "read" information from a picture and tell adult why he or she thinks as he or she does. For example, a teacher asks why the child in the picture is sad, the child looks at the picture of a child with a scraped knee and says, "He hurt his knee."*	0 1 2		
4.4 Makes predictions when reading a story *Child makes predictions about what will happen in the story. For example, a teacher asks, "I wonder what will happen to Sam?" and the child predicts what will happen to Sam.*	0 1 2		
4.5 Identifies letters—receptively *Child identifies all the letters in the alphabet, receptively.*	0 1 2		
4.6 Identifies letters—expressively *Child identifies all the letters in the alphabet, expressively.*	0 1 2		

5. Emergent math	Scoring	Comments	*
5.1 Demonstrates concept of one *When given several items, child gives or assigns one item when asked to do so. For example, child gives one cup to each student during snack, or child gives one cup to you when asked to do so.*	0 1 2		
5.2 Counting objects with one-to-one correspondence *Child counts at least ten items.*	0 1 2		

Summary notes for cognitive

D. COMMUNICATION

DATA

1. Following directions	Scoring	Comments	*
1.1 Follows one-step directions without contextual cues *For example, adult tells the child, "Get the ball" when it is not immediately present; child gets the ball. Child must be able to follow at least five different simple directions.*	0 1 2		
1.2 Follows one-step directions related to safety *For example: hold hands, stop, wait, hands down, walk with me. Child must be able to follow at least four different directions.*	0 1 2		
1.3 Follows directions to give an item to a person *When given an item, the child will follow the direction, such as "Go give Jeremy the ball."*	0 1 2		
1.4 Follows two-step directions without contextual cues *When doll is not present in immediate environment and an adult or peer tells the child, "Go get your doll and put it on the table," child will follow both directions in order without reminders. Child must be able to follow at least four different two-step directions.*	0 1 2		
2. Responding	**Scoring**	**Comments**	*****
2.1 Gestures or vocalizes to greet others *Child waves arm or vocalizes when greeting and when leaving others.*	0 1 2		
2.2 Chooses item when asked to make a choice *Present two items and ask child to choose. Child must indicate preferred choice by then taking the item and acting upon it.*	0 1 2		
2.3 Responds to question "What do you want?" when items are not present *Child is not able to see preferred items but will request them when asked.*	0 1 2		
2.4 Responds to a variety of questions			
■ What	0 1 2		
■ Where	0 1 2		
■ Who	0 1 2		
■ Why	0 1 2		
■ When	0 1 2		
Child must be able to respond to three different types of questions for each one listed above.	0 1 2		
2.5 Responds with a yes or no answer			
■ When asked, "Do you want _____?"	0 1 2		
■ When asked, "Is this a cow?" *Child must be able to answer both yes and no.*	0 1 2		

3.	Initiating	Scoring	Comments	*
3.1	Uses gestures to initiate a request *For example, pointing to items out of reach*	0 1 2		
3.2	Initiates with words or gestures to greet others *For example, child waves or says "Hi."*	0 1 2		
3.3	Requests items or activities that are in sight *Child must request a variety of preferred items when child can see the items.*	0 1 2		
3.4	Requests items or activities that are out of sight *Child must request a variety of preferred items that are not visible to the child.*	0 1 2		
3.5	Requests the end of an activity *Child will ask to be "All done" or "Finished" after working with an activity.*	0 1 2		
3.6	Makes comments *During activities, child makes simple comments such as "I'm drawing" during an art activity or "Baby crying" during play.*	0 1 2		
3.7	Uses sentence stems, such as "I want ____," "It's a ____," "I see ____," and "I have ____" to comment and request *Child says a variety of sentences with each sentence stem.*	0 1 2		
3.8	Asks a variety of questions to gain more information			
	■ What (e.g., what is that)	0 1 2		
	■ Where (e.g., where are the markers)	0 1 2		
	■ Who (e.g., who is that)	0 1 2		
	■ Why (e.g., why is she crying)	0 1 2		
	■ When (e.g., when are we going)	0 1 2		
	Child must be able to initiate three different types of questions for each one listed above.			

4.	Comprehension and expression of words and sentences	Receptive	Expressive	Comments	*
4.1	Identifies at least 50 common nouns in pictures and the environment *For example, child points to a ball or truck in pictures from an array of at least three. Child names objects in pictures spontaneously or when asked.*	0 1 2	0 1 2		
4.2	Identifies at least 15 actions in pictures and the environment *For example, when looking at a book or pictures out on table, teacher says, "Who is jumping?" or "Show me reading" and child indicates correct answer When a teacher asks, "What is he or she doing?" child names action.*	0 1 2	0 1 2		
4.3	Uses pronouns *Child must use a variety of pronouns that may include me, mine, I, you, my, and this.*	0 1 2	0 1 2		

4.	Comprehension and expression of words and sentences (*continued*)	Receptive	Expressive	Comments	*
4.4	Identifies at least 10 functions across a variety of common objects or pictures *For example, teacher puts out three different objects or pictures and asks, "Which one do you eat?" "Which one do you play with?" "Which one do you read?" Child fills in the blank when asked, "You eat with a _____?"*	0 1 2	0 1 2		
4.5	Identifies at least 10 features across a variety of common objects or pictures *For example, teacher puts out three different objects or pictures and asks questions such as, "Which one has a tail?" and "Which one has wheels?" Child fills in the blank when a teacher says, "A bird has a _____."*	0 1 2	0 1 2		
4.6	Identifies at least five categories across a variety of common objects or pictures within each category *For example, teacher puts out objects or pictures and asks questions such as, "Which one is an animal?" "Which one is a food?" Child fills in the blank when a teacher says, "This is a kind of _____."*	0 1 2	0 1 2		
4.7	Identifies and uses a variety of attributes				
	■ Colors	0 1 2	0 1 2		
	■ Sizes	0 1 2	0 1 2		
	■ Shapes	0 1 2	0 1 2		
	■ ____________________	0 1 2	0 1 2		
	For example, teacher puts out several blocks, different only by color and asks "Give me the green block." When requesting an item, child uses modifiers, such as "I want the big block."				
4.8	Identifies and uses prepositions *For example, teacher asks the child "Which car is under the bridge?" or "Give me the car that is on the bridge?" Additionally, teacher may request "Where is the train?" and the child responds "Under the bridge." Child must identify a variety of prepositions.*	0 1 2	0 1 2		

Summary notes for communication

E. SOCIAL

DATA

1. **Joint attention**		**Scoring**	**Comments**	*
1.1	References communicative partner during a social-communicative interaction *For example, adult looks surprised and child reacts. Child looks at peer when responding to a request.*	0 1 2		
1.2	Follows pointing gesture to establish joint attention *Child looks in the direction of a person's pointing gesture while that person looks at an object, person, or event and comments on it. Child's glance must be longer than 1 second.*	0 1 2		
1.3	Follows gaze to establish joint attention *Child looks in direction of person's gaze while person looks at object, person, or event. Child's glance must be longer than 1 second.*	0 1 2		
1.4	Initiates gestures to establish joint attention *For example, points to a picture when looking at a book; child points to other children playing.*	0 1 2		
1.5	Initiates gaze to establish joint attention *For example, looks at a child crying and then looks at adult.*	0 1 2		
1.6	Maintains a social-communicative interaction with an adult for two exchanges *Consider developmentally appropriate interactions. Interactions may range from peek-a-boo to a conversation.*	0 1 2		
2.	**Pragmatic rules**	**Scoring**	**Comments**	*
2.1	Maintains appropriate proximity to conversation partner *The child does not stand too close or touch other person.*	0 1 2		
2.2	Orients body towards speaker *During a conversation, the child turns their body to the other person.*	0 1 2		
2.3	Maintains eye contact *During a conversation, the child looks in the direction of the other person.*	0 1 2		
2.4	Uses voice volume appropriate to setting *When inside a building, does not talk loudly.*	0 1 2		
2.5	Responds appropriately to common facial expressions and gestures (e.g., head nod and shake) *For example, if adult shakes head to indicate no, the child responds accordingly.*	0 1 2		
2.6	Appropriately interjects *During a conversation, the child waits for a pause and then says "Excuse me," "Guess what," or "Do you know what I did?"*			
2.7	Ends the conversation appropriately *When the conversation is over the child says, "I have to go now" or "See you later."*	0 1 2		

3. Interactions with peers	Scoring	Comments	*
3.1 Maintains proximity to peers *Child stays within three feet of peers when playing in an unstructured setting.*	0 1 2		
3.2 Imitates peers *For example, when peer is clapping hands in circle, child imitates actions, when peer says, "hip, hip, hooray,, child says, or approximates, the same.*	0 1 2		
3.3 Takes turns with peers *For example, rolling ball back and forth, taking turns with toys. Child will follow direction of an adult to take a turn by offering toy to friend, waiting, and then taking toy again when it is his or her turn.*	0 1 2		
3.4 Responds to interactions from peers *For example, physically accepts toy from peer, answers question.*	0 1 2		
3.5 Initiates interactions towards peers *For example, offers a toy, spontaneously requests an object*	0 1 2		
3.6 Takes turns during unstructured activities *When playing with art materials that are limited, the child will wait for a turn for the scissors.* *When playing grocery store in dramatic play, the child will wait for turn to be the cashier and will provide opportunity for another child to be cashier.*	0 1 2		
3.7 Demonstrates acceptable ways of joining an activity *Observes peers at playing with blocks and asks to join in "Can I play?" or offers a block to put on the structure they are building.*	0 1 2		
3.8 Maintains a conversation with a peer *Child continues a communicative interaction with a peer by asking questions and making comments for at least three turns.*	0 1 2		
3.9 Gives assistance to peers *If a peer is trying to get a toy to work, the child will try to help them.*	0 1 2		

Summary notes for social

F. PLAY

DATA

1.	**Play fundamentals**	**Scoring**	**Comments**	*****
1.1	Activates cause and effect toys *Cause and effect toys may include jack-in-the-box, wind-up radio, See-N-Say*	0 1 2		
1.2	Uses play materials appropriately *Child acts on objects using functionally or socially appropriate actions. Functionally or socially appropriate actions are those for which the object was intended or designed (e.g., child holds play telephone to ear, puts comb to head and attempts to comb hair, puts glasses on eyes).*	0 1 2		
1.3	Demonstrates functional play with toys related to play theme *For example, feeds baby, brushes baby's teeth, and puts the baby to bed. Child only needs to demonstrate each functional play action; the actions do not need to be in order or sustained.*	0 1 2		
1.4	Uses representational actions with objects *For example, child uses a box as a hat, a spoon as a telephone, a stick to stir food.*	0 1 2		
1.5	Completes a sequence of pretend play actions related to play theme *With dramatic play materials, child may prepare food with the kitchen set, set the table, and place the food on the table. Child must be able to play with a variety of toys across sequences of play themes.*	0 1 2		
1.6	Narrates play *Child describes or states what he or she is doing with play materials.*	0 1 2		
2.	**Independent play**	**Scoring**	**Comments**	*****
2.1	Entertains self by playing appropriately with toys for at least 5 minutes *Child can choose toy or be given toys.*	0 1 2		
2.2	Completes puzzles *Child completes puzzles as developmentally appropriate. Consider inset, inset interlocking, and jigsaw puzzles.*	0 1 2		
2.3	Colors or draws *Child uses drawing or writing materials as developmentally appropriate. Consider scribbling, circles, lines, and drawing simple shapes and designs (e.g., a happy face).*	0 1 2		
2.4	Begins and completes at least three different age appropriate activities independently *For example, child chooses a book, looks at it, puts it away.*	0 1 2		
3.	**Interactive play**	**Scoring**	**Comments**	*****
3.1	Engages in parallel play *Child plays with farm materials near peer playing with animals. Child plays with dollhouse materials while peer plays with dollhouse.*	0 1 2		
3.2	Engages in associative play *Child plays with same materials, but child(ren) may have different agendas or goals about play. Children do not have to carry out same activity, but are playing on same toys. Children not working toward same goals as in cooperative play.*	0 1 2		

3. Interactive play (*continued*)	Scoring	Comments	*
3.3 Makes comments about own play to peers *When drawing will remark to a peer, "I am drawing a train" or when building playing with plastic animals will comment, "The shark is swimming in the ocean."*	0 1 2		
3.4 Organizes play by suggesting a play plan *Might suggest, "Let's make a train track and then drive the trains."*	0 1 2		
3.5 Follow a peer's play idea *If peer suggests making a train track and driving trains, the child will join the play to make a track.*	0 1 2		
3.6 Plays cooperatively *Take on pretend role during dramatic play, lead the play by offering play suggestions to peers, and follow game with rules.*	0 1 2		
3.7 Plays games with rules until end of game *Child plays at least three different games, including board games, with only minimal adult supervision.*	0 1 2		

Summary notes for play

PRIORITY SKILLS/BEHAVIORS TO BE ADDRESSED

Adaptive
1.
2.
3.

Executive Functioning
1.
2.
3.

Cognitive
1.
2.
3.

Communication
1.
2.
3.

Social
1.
2.
3.

Play
1.
2.
3.

DO NOT BREAK.

These forms are not sold individually. They are available only as a set. Resellers should not open shrink-wrapped sets.

ISBN-13: 978-1-68125-220-9
ISBN-10: 1-68125-220-1